Forex Trading 101: A Beginner's Guide to Mastering the Market

Forex Freddy

Dedication

To all the aspiring forex traders out there, may this book be the start of your journey to financial independence and success. May you find the knowledge and strategies within these pages helpful in achieving your trading goals. This book is dedicated to you and your dreams of a better future.

Table of contents

Next Steps for Beginner Traders
Additional Resources for Learning and Improvement.

Chapter 1: Introduction

What is forex trading

Forex trading, also known as foreign exchange trading or currency trading, is the buying and selling of currencies in the global foreign exchange market. The forex market is the largest financial market in the world, with an average daily trading volume of over $6 trillion. Forex trading allows individuals, institutions, and governments to exchange one currency for another, with the goal of making a profit from the exchange rate fluctuations between two currencies.

Forex trading takes place on a decentralized network of electronic platforms that operate 24 hours a day, five days a week, across different time zones around the world. Trading in the forex market involves buying and selling currency pairs, such as EUR/USD, USD/JPY, GBP/USD, and many more. When you buy a currency pair, you are buying the base currency and selling the quote currency. When you sell a currency pair, you are selling the base currency and buying the quote currency.

Forex trading is based on the concept of currency exchange rates, which determine the value of one currency in relation to another currency. Exchange rates are influenced by a range of economic and political factors, including interest rates, inflation, geopolitical events, and global trade. Forex traders use fundamental and technical analysis to assess market conditions and make trading decisions. Fundamental analysis involves analyzing economic and political factors that may impact exchange rates, while technical analysis involves using charts and technical indicators to identify trends and patterns in price movements.

Forex trading offers numerous opportunities for traders to profit from exchange rate movements, but it also involves significant risks. Traders must be knowledgeable and disciplined to succeed in the forex market. It is important to have a sound trading strategy, effective risk management techniques, and a solid understanding of the factors that affect exchange rates. With the right education and training, forex trading can be a lucrative and exciting activity for those who are willing to put in the time and effort to learn.

The advantages of forex trading

Forex trading offers several advantages to individuals, institutions, and governments who participate in the market. Here are some of the key advantages of forex trading:

Liquidity: The forex market is the most liquid financial market in the world, with an average daily trading volume of over $6 trillion. This means that traders can enter and exit positions quickly and easily, even in large sizes, without affecting the exchange rates significantly.

Accessibility: Forex trading is open to anyone with an internet connection, making it accessible to individuals from all over the world. Unlike other financial markets that require large amounts of capital to get started, forex trading can be done with a relatively small amount of money.

Flexibility: The forex market is open 24 hours a day, five days a week, allowing traders to participate in the market at their convenience. This flexibility makes it easier for traders to balance their trading activities with their personal and professional lives.

Volatility: The forex market is highly volatile, which means that there are opportunities to profit from large price movements. Traders can take advantage of short-term price fluctuations and can also hold positions for longer periods to benefit from longer-term trends.

Diversification: Forex trading provides traders with an opportunity to diversify their portfolio, as it is not closely correlated with other financial markets such as stocks, bonds, and commodities. This can help to reduce overall portfolio risk.

Leverage: Forex brokers offer traders leverage, which means that they can control a larger position with a smaller amount of capital. This can amplify profits, but it also increases the risk of losses, so it should be used with caution.

In conclusion, forex trading offers several advantages to traders, including liquidity, accessibility, flexibility, volatility, diversification, and leverage. However, traders should be aware of the risks involved and should have a sound trading strategy and risk management plan in place.

The risks of forex trading

Forex trading is a highly leveraged and volatile financial market, and as such, it is important to be aware of the risks involved. Here are some of the key risks associated with forex trading:

High Volatility: The forex market is highly volatile, which means that exchange rates can fluctuate rapidly and unpredictably. This volatility can lead to significant price movements in short periods, and it can be challenging to predict these movements accurately.

Leverage: Forex trading involves using leverage, which means that traders can control large positions with a small amount of capital. While leverage can amplify profits, it can also amplify losses. If a trader uses too much leverage, a small price movement can result in a significant loss.

Market Risk: Forex trading is subject to market risks, which can arise from a range of factors such as changes in interest rates, economic data releases, geopolitical events, and central bank policies. These factors can impact exchange rates and cause unexpected price movements.

Counterparty Risk: Forex trading is conducted through a network of brokers, banks, and other financial institutions. There is always a risk that one of these counterparties may default on their obligations, which can lead to losses for traders.

Technology Risk: Forex trading is heavily reliant on technology, and there is a risk of technical failures or disruptions that can impact trading activities. This can include issues such as platform outages, connectivity problems, and data feed issues.

Psychological Risk: Forex trading can be emotionally challenging, and there is a risk of making irrational decisions due to fear, greed, or other emotions. Traders need to have the discipline and emotional control to stick to their trading plan and manage their risk effectively.

In conclusion, forex trading involves significant risks, and traders need to be aware of these risks and have a sound risk management plan in place. This can include strategies such as limiting leverage, using stop-loss orders, diversifying their portfolio, and maintaining a disciplined trading approach. By understanding the risks and taking appropriate measures to manage them, traders can minimize their losses and maximize their chances of success in the forex market.

The history of forex trading

Forex trading has a long and fascinating history that spans several centuries. Here is a brief overview of the history of forex trading:

Origins of Currency Trading: Currency trading can be traced back to ancient times when traders exchanged goods and services with each other using different forms of currency. As international trade expanded, merchants began using standardized forms of currency, such as gold and silver coins, to facilitate transactions.

Bretton Woods Agreement: Following World War II, the Bretton Woods Agreement was signed in 1944, which established a fixed exchange rate system for major currencies. The US dollar was fixed to gold, and other currencies were fixed to the US dollar. This system remained in place until 1971 when the US abandoned the gold standard.

Floating Exchange Rates: After the collapse of the Bretton Woods system, major currencies began to float freely against each other, and the foreign exchange market emerged as a global market for currency trading. Advances in technology, such as the internet and electronic trading platforms, have made it easier for individuals and institutions to participate in the forex market.

Globalization and Market Size: The growth of international trade, investment, and tourism has led to an increase in the volume of currency transactions. The forex market is now the largest financial market in the world, with an average daily trading volume of over $6 trillion.

Regulatory Changes: The forex market has undergone several regulatory changes over the years to improve transparency, protect investors, and prevent market manipulation. In recent years, regulators have focused on improving the quality of execution and reducing the impact of conflicts of interest between brokers and traders.

Evolution of Trading Strategies: The history of forex trading has also seen the evolution of trading strategies and techniques, from simple charting and technical analysis to complex algorithms and machine learning. Traders have developed a range of approaches, including fundamental analysis, technical analysis, and quantitative analysis, to analyze market data and make trading decisions.

In conclusion, forex trading has a rich and complex history that reflects the evolution of global commerce and financial markets. The forex market continues to evolve, driven by advances in technology and changes in regulatory and market conditions.

Chapter 2: Understanding forex trading concepts

Currency pairs and exchange rates

Currency pairs and exchange rates are two essential concepts in forex trading. Here's what you need to know:

Currency Pairs: In forex trading, currencies are traded in pairs, with the first currency in the pair called the "base currency," and the second currency is the "quote currency." For example, in the currency pair EUR/USD, the euro is the base currency, and the US dollar is the quote currency. Currency pairs are quoted as bid and ask prices, which represent the price at which traders can buy or sell the currency pair.

Exchange Rates: The exchange rate is the price at which one currency can be exchanged for another currency. Exchange rates are influenced by a range of factors, including economic data, central bank policies, geopolitical events, and market sentiment. In the forex market, exchange rates are constantly changing, reflecting the supply and demand for different currencies.

Major Currency Pairs: The most actively traded currency pairs in the forex market are known as the "major currency pairs." These include EUR/USD, USD/JPY, GBP/USD, USD/CHF, AUD/USD, and USD/CAD. These pairs are highly liquid, with tight bid-ask spreads, and are popular with traders due to their high trading volumes and volatility.

Cross Currency Pairs: Cross currency pairs, also known as "minor currency pairs," are currency pairs that do not include the US dollar. These pairs are less liquid and less frequently traded than major currency pairs. Examples of cross currency pairs include EUR/GBP, EUR/JPY, and AUD/JPY.

Exchange Rate Factors: Exchange rates are influenced by a range of factors, including economic data, political developments, and central bank policies. For example, a country with strong economic data, such as high GDP growth or low unemployment, is likely to have a strong currency. Similarly, a central bank that raises interest rates is likely to attract foreign investment and strengthen its currency.

In conclusion, understanding currency pairs and exchange rates is essential for successful forex trading. Traders need to keep up-to-date with the latest economic and political developments that can impact exchange rates, and use technical and fundamental analysis to make informed trading decisions. By understanding the dynamics of currency pairs and exchange rates, traders can increase their chances of success in the forex market.

Pips and pipettes

Pips and pipettes are units of measurement used in forex trading to express changes in the value of a currency pair. Here's what you need to know:

Pips: A pip, short for "percentage in point," is the smallest unit of measurement in forex trading. One pip represents the fourth decimal place in a currency pair's exchange rate. For example, if the exchange rate for the EUR/USD pair changes from 1.1234 to 1.1235, this represents a one-pip change.

Pipettes: A pipette, also known as a "fractional pip," is a unit of measurement that represents one-tenth of a pip. It is used when brokers quote exchange rates to five decimal places instead of four. For example, if the exchange rate for the EUR/USD pair changes from 1.12345 to 1.12346, this represents a one-pipette change.

Pip Values: The value of a pip depends on the size of the trade and the currency pair being traded. For example, the value of one pip for a standard lot of EUR/USD (100,000 units) is $10. Similarly, the value of one pip for a mini lot of EUR/USD (10,000 units) is $1. Traders can use pip calculators to determine the value of pips for different currency pairs and lot sizes.

Pip Spreads: In addition to pip values, traders also need to consider pip spreads, which are the difference between the bid and ask prices for a currency pair. The pip spread represents the cost of trading and can vary depending on market conditions and broker policies. Tight pip spreads can be advantageous for traders as they reduce the cost of trading.

Pip Accuracy: While pips and pipettes are commonly used to express changes in exchange rates, they are not always accurate representations of market movements. Forex prices can fluctuate rapidly, and a small change in the exchange rate may represent a significant movement in the value of a trade. Therefore, traders should use pips and pipettes as a general guide and supplement their analysis with other indicators and tools.

In conclusion, understanding pips and pipettes is essential for successful forex trading. Traders need to be aware of the value of pips and pipettes for different currency pairs and lot sizes, as well as the impact of pip spreads on trading costs. By using pips and pipettes as part of a broader trading strategy, traders can better manage risk and make more informed trading decisions.

Lot sizes and leverage

Lot sizes and leverage are two important concepts in forex trading that can significantly impact a trader's profitability and risk exposure. Here's what you need to know:

Lot Sizes: A lot is a standardized unit of measurement used in forex trading to represent the size of a trade. There are three main types of lot sizes: standard lots, mini lots, and micro lots. A standard lot is equal to 100,000 units of the base currency, a mini lot is equal to 10,000 units, and a micro lot is equal to 1,000 units. Choosing the appropriate lot size is essential for managing risk and ensuring that a trader has sufficient margin to cover potential losses.

Leverage: Leverage is a tool that allows traders to control larger positions in the market with a smaller amount of capital. For example, a leverage ratio of 1:100 means that a trader can control a position worth $100,000 with just $1,000 in their trading account. Leverage can magnify gains and losses, and traders need to be careful when using high leverage ratios to avoid overexposure and margin calls.

Margin: Margin is the amount of money that a trader needs to maintain in their trading account to keep their positions open. Margin is typically expressed as a percentage of the total trade size and is required to cover potential losses. Margin requirements vary depending on the broker and the currency pair being traded, and traders need to be aware of their margin requirements at all times to avoid being closed out of positions.

Risk Management: Choosing the appropriate lot size and leverage ratio is essential for managing risk in forex trading. Traders need to have a clear understanding of their risk tolerance and use appropriate risk management techniques, such as setting stop-loss orders and limiting the amount of capital they risk on each trade.

Regulation: Lot sizes and leverage ratios are subject to regulation in many countries to protect retail traders from excessive risk. Traders need to be aware of the regulatory environment in their country and the requirements of their broker to ensure that they are trading in compliance with the law.

In conclusion, lot sizes and leverage are important concepts in forex trading that can significantly impact a trader's profitability and risk exposure. Traders need to choose appropriate lot sizes and leverage ratios, manage their risk effectively, and be aware of the regulatory environment in their country to ensure successful trading.

Margin and margin calls

Margin is the amount of money that a trader needs to maintain in their trading account to keep their positions open. When a trader enters into a leveraged trade, the broker will require a certain amount of margin as a percentage of the total trade size. This margin is essentially a deposit that the trader needs to maintain in their trading account to cover potential losses.

Margin is calculated based on the size of the position, the leverage ratio, and the currency pair being traded. Different brokers have different margin requirements, and margin requirements can also vary depending on the volatility of the market.

Margin calls occur when a trader's account falls below the required margin level. This can happen if the market moves against the trader's position, causing losses to accumulate. If the losses become too large and the trader's account falls below the required margin level, the broker will issue a margin call.

A margin call requires the trader to deposit more funds into their trading account to bring the account balance back up to the required margin level. If the trader does not respond to the margin call, the broker may close out some or all of the trader's positions to reduce their exposure and recover the funds that the trader owes.

Margin calls can be a serious risk for traders, as they can lead to significant losses and potentially wipe out the entire trading account. To avoid margin calls, traders need to manage their risk effectively and use appropriate position sizing and risk management techniques, such as setting stop-loss orders and limiting the amount of capital they risk on each trade.

In summary, margin is the amount of money that a trader needs to maintain in their trading account to keep their positions open. Margin calls occur when a trader's account falls below the required margin level, and traders need to manage their risk effectively to avoid margin calls and protect their trading capital.

Chapter 3: Fundamental analysis

Economic indicators and their impact on currency markets

Economic indicators are statistics that provide insights into the health and performance of an economy. In forex trading, economic indicators are closely watched by traders as they can have a significant impact on currency markets.

Here are some of the most important economic indicators and their impact on currency markets:

Gross Domestic Product (GDP): GDP is the total value of all goods and services produced in a country in a given period. A higher GDP indicates a stronger economy, which can be positive for the currency. However, if the GDP growth rate is too high, it can lead to inflation, which can be negative for the currency.

Inflation: Inflation is the rate at which prices of goods and services increase. High inflation can lead to a decrease in the value of a currency as the purchasing power of that currency declines. Central banks often use monetary policy tools, such as interest rate adjustments, to control inflation.

Interest Rates: Interest rates are the rates at which banks lend money to each other. Higher interest rates can attract foreign investment, which can increase demand for the currency and lead to appreciation. On the other hand, lower interest rates can make a currency less attractive and lead to depreciation.

Employment Data: Employment data, such as the nonfarm payroll report in the United States, can provide insights into the health of an economy. A higher-than-expected employment rate can be positive for the currency, while a lower-than-expected rate can be negative.

Trade Balance: The trade balance measures the difference between a country's exports and imports. A positive trade balance, where exports exceed imports, can be positive for the currency as it indicates a strong economy. However, a negative trade balance can lead to a weaker currency.

Traders use economic indicators to analyze market trends and make informed trading decisions. By understanding the impact of these indicators on currency markets, traders can identify potential trading opportunities and manage their risk effectively. It is important to note that economic indicators can be unpredictable, and unexpected events can have a significant impact on currency markets. Traders should always keep an eye on the news and be prepared to adjust their trading strategies as needed.

News releases and their effect on currency prices

News releases are important events that can have a significant impact on currency prices. Economic news releases are typically released by governments, central banks, or other organizations, and provide information about economic performance or policy decisions.

Here are some of the most important news releases and their potential impact on currency prices:

Interest Rate Decisions: When a central bank announces a change in interest rates, it can have a significant impact on currency prices. A higher interest rate can increase demand for a currency, while a lower interest rate can decrease demand.

Gross Domestic Product (GDP) Releases: GDP releases can provide insights into the overall health of an economy. A better-than-expected GDP release can lead to appreciation of the currency, while a worse-than-expected release can lead to depreciation.

Employment Reports: Employment reports, such as nonfarm payrolls in the United States, can provide insights into the strength of an economy. A better-than-expected employment report can lead to appreciation of the currency, while a worse-than-expected report can lead to depreciation.

Inflation Reports: Inflation reports, such as the Consumer Price Index (CPI), can provide insights into the inflation rate and purchasing power of a currency. Higher-than-expected inflation can lead to appreciation of the currency, while lower-than-expected inflation can lead to depreciation.

Political Developments: Political developments, such as elections or policy changes, can also have a significant impact on currency prices. Changes in government or policy can lead to uncertainty, which can lead to depreciation of the currency.

Traders need to stay up-to-date with news releases and understand their potential impact on currency prices. It is important to note that news releases can be unpredictable, and unexpected events can occur. Traders should always manage their risk effectively by using appropriate position sizing and risk management techniques, such as setting stop-loss orders and limiting the amount of capital they risk on each trade.

Central banks and monetary policy

Central banks play a crucial role in the forex market through their monetary policy decisions. Monetary policy refers to the actions taken by a central bank to influence the availability and cost of money and credit in an economy.

Here are some of the key tools and strategies used by central banks in their monetary policy:

Interest Rates: Central banks use interest rates to control the supply of money in the economy. By raising or lowering interest rates, a central bank can influence borrowing and lending behavior, which can affect economic growth and inflation.

Reserve Requirements: Central banks can require banks to hold a certain percentage of their deposits in reserve. By increasing or decreasing reserve requirements, a central bank can influence the amount of money that banks have available for lending.

Open Market Operations: Central banks can buy or sell government securities in the open market to influence the supply of money and credit. By buying securities, a central bank can increase the amount of money in circulation, while selling securities can decrease the money supply.

Forward Guidance: Central banks can use forward guidance to provide information about their future policy intentions. By signaling their plans, central banks can influence market expectations and help to guide economic behavior.

The monetary policy decisions made by central banks can have a significant impact on currency markets. For example, if a central bank raises interest rates, it can make the currency more attractive to foreign investors, which can lead to appreciation. On the other hand, if a central bank lowers interest rates, it can make the currency less attractive, which can lead to depreciation.

Traders need to closely monitor the monetary policy decisions made by central banks and their potential impact on currency markets. By staying up-to-date with the latest news and using technical analysis to analyze market trends, traders can identify potential trading opportunities and manage their risk effectively.

Geopolitical events and their influence on currency markets

Geopolitical events can have a significant impact on currency markets, as they can create uncertainty and affect the perceived strength of a country's economy. Here are some examples of geopolitical events that can influence currency markets:

Wars and Conflicts: Wars and conflicts can have a significant impact on currency markets, as they can create instability and uncertainty. For example, during the Gulf War in the early 1990s, the value of the U.S. dollar initially fell as investors became concerned about the impact of the conflict on the U.S. economy.

Political Instability: Political instability, such as changes in government or political crises, can also affect currency markets. For example, in 2016, the value of the British pound fell sharply after the United Kingdom voted to leave the European Union in a referendum known as "Brexit."

Natural Disasters: Natural disasters, such as earthquakes or hurricanes, can also have an impact on currency markets. For example, after the 2011 earthquake and tsunami in Japan, the value of the Japanese yen initially fell as investors became concerned about the impact of the disaster on the Japanese economy.

Trade Disputes: Trade disputes between countries can also influence currency markets. For example, in 2018, the United States and China engaged in a trade war that led to the imposition of tariffs on goods, which affected the value of both the U.S. dollar and the Chinese yuan.

Traders need to stay up-to-date with geopolitical events and their potential impact on currency markets. By monitoring news and analyzing market trends, traders can identify potential trading opportunities and manage their risk effectively. It is important to note that geopolitical events can be unpredictable, and unexpected events can occur. Therefore, traders should always be prepared to adapt their trading strategies and manage their risk appropriately.

Chapter 4: Technical analysis

Candlestick charts and patterns

Candlestick charts are a popular type of chart used in forex trading to analyze market trends and make trading decisions. A candlestick chart displays the price movements of a currency pair over a specific period of time, such as one hour or one day. Each candlestick on the chart represents a specific time period and contains information about the opening, closing, high, and low prices of the currency pair for that period.

Candlestick patterns are formations of one or more candlesticks on a chart that can indicate potential changes in market trends. Here are some common candlestick patterns:

Doji: A doji is a candlestick with a small body and long wicks on both ends. It indicates that the opening and closing prices of the currency pair were very close, which can signal indecision in the market.

Hammer: A hammer is a candlestick with a small body and a long lower wick. It can indicate a potential reversal in a downtrend, as buyers are stepping in to support the price.

Shooting Star: A shooting star is a candlestick with a small body and a long upper wick. It can indicate a potential reversal in an uptrend, as sellers are stepping in to push the price down.

Engulfing: An engulfing pattern is when one candlestick completely engulfs the body of the previous candlestick. It can indicate a potential reversal in the market trend.

Traders use candlestick charts and patterns to identify potential trading opportunities and manage their risk effectively. By analyzing patterns and trends on the chart, traders can make more informed decisions about when to enter or exit a trade. It is important to note that candlestick patterns should not be used in isolation and should be considered in conjunction with other technical and fundamental analysis tools.

Trend lines and channels

Trend lines and channels are technical analysis tools used in forex trading to identify and analyze trends in the market. A trend line is a straight line that connects two or more price points on a chart, while a channel is a range of prices between two parallel trend lines.

Trend lines are used to identify the direction of the trend in a currency pair. An uptrend is characterized by a series of higher highs and higher lows, while a downtrend is characterized by a series of lower highs and lower lows. Traders draw trend lines by connecting the lows in an uptrend or the highs in a downtrend. When the price breaks through the trend line, it can indicate a potential reversal in the trend.

Channels are used to identify the range of prices within which a currency pair is trading. Traders draw two parallel trend lines, one above and one below the price action, to create a channel. When the price reaches the upper or lower trend line, it can indicate a potential resistance or support level.

Traders use trend lines and channels to identify potential trading opportunities and manage their risk effectively. By analyzing the direction of the trend and the range of prices within which a currency pair is trading, traders can make more informed decisions about when to enter or exit a trade. It is important to note that trend lines and channels should be used in conjunction with other technical and fundamental analysis tools, and should be updated regularly to reflect changes in the market.

Support and resistance levels

Support and resistance levels are important technical analysis tools used in forex trading to identify potential price levels at which a currency pair may encounter buying or selling pressure. Support levels are price levels at which the demand for a currency pair is strong enough to prevent the price from falling further, while resistance levels are price levels at which the supply of a currency pair is strong enough to prevent the price from rising further.

Support and resistance levels can be identified by analyzing price charts and identifying areas where the price has previously found support or resistance. When the price approaches a support or resistance level, traders look for signs of a potential reversal or continuation of the trend. For example, if the price approaches a support level and bounces off of it, it may indicate a potential buying opportunity. On the other hand, if the price approaches a resistance level and fails to break through it, it may indicate a potential selling opportunity.

Traders use support and resistance levels to identify potential trading opportunities and manage their risk effectively. By analyzing the levels at which a currency pair may encounter buying or selling pressure, traders can make more informed decisions about when to enter or exit a trade. It is important to note that support and resistance levels should be used in conjunction with other technical and fundamental analysis tools, and should be updated regularly to reflect changes in the market.

Common technical indicators

There are numerous technical indicators used in forex trading, but some of the most commonly used include:

Moving Averages: A moving average is a popular indicator used to identify trends in the market. It calculates the average price of a currency pair over a specified period of time, such as 10 days or 50 days. Traders use moving averages to identify the direction of the trend and potential support and resistance levels.

Relative Strength Index (RSI): The RSI is a momentum indicator that measures the strength of a currency pair's price action. It compares the average gain and loss of a currency pair over a specified period of time, such as 14 days. Traders use the RSI to identify potential overbought or oversold conditions and potential reversal points.

Bollinger Bands: Bollinger Bands are a volatility indicator that uses a moving average and two standard deviations to create a range around the price of a currency pair. Traders use Bollinger Bands to identify potential support and resistance levels and to gauge the volatility of the market.

Stochastic Oscillator: The stochastic oscillator is a momentum indicator that compares the current price of a currency pair to its range over a specified period of time. Traders use the stochastic oscillator to identify potential overbought or oversold conditions and potential reversal points.

Fibonacci Retracement: Fibonacci retracement is a tool that uses horizontal lines to identify potential support and resistance levels based on the Fibonacci sequence, a mathematical pattern found in nature. Traders use Fibonacci retracement to identify potential entry and exit points and to gauge the strength of the trend.

Traders use these and other technical indicators to identify potential trading opportunities and manage their risk effectively. It is important to note that technical indicators should be used in conjunction with other technical and fundamental analysis tools, and should be updated regularly to reflect changes in the market.

Chapter 5: Risk management

Setting stop-loss and take-profit orders

Setting stop-loss and take-profit orders is an important part of forex trading risk management. A stop-loss order is an order to close a trade at a predetermined price if the market moves against the trader's position. A take-profit order is an order to close a trade at a predetermined price if the market moves in favor of the trader's position.

Stop-loss orders help traders limit their losses by closing a trade automatically if the market moves against them beyond a certain point. Traders should set their stop-loss orders at a level that allows for some market volatility, but also limits the potential loss on a trade to a level they are comfortable with.

Take-profit orders help traders lock in profits by closing a trade automatically when the market moves in their favor beyond a certain point. Traders should set their take-profit orders at a level that allows for some market volatility, but also takes advantage of potential profit opportunities.

When setting stop-loss and take-profit orders, traders should consider their trading strategy, risk tolerance, and the current market conditions. Traders should also monitor their trades regularly to ensure that their stop-loss and take-profit levels remain appropriate and adjust them as necessary.

It is important to note that stop-loss and take-profit orders do not guarantee that a trade will be closed at the desired price. In fast-moving markets, the price may move beyond the stop-loss or take-profit level before the order can be executed. Traders should also be aware that setting stop-loss and take-profit orders too close to the current market price may result in premature order execution, which may lead to missed profit opportunities or increased losses.

Risk/reward ratio

The risk/reward ratio is a commonly used concept in forex trading that compares the potential profit of a trade to the potential loss. The risk/reward ratio is calculated by dividing the potential profit by the potential loss. For example, if a trader expects to make a profit of $500 on a trade and their potential loss is $200, the risk/reward ratio would be 2.5:1 ($500/$200).

The risk/reward ratio is an important consideration for traders because it helps them determine if a trade is worth taking based on the potential reward relative to the potential risk. A risk/reward ratio of 1:1 means that the potential profit is equal to the potential loss, while a ratio of 2:1 means that the potential profit is twice the potential loss.

Traders generally aim for a risk/reward ratio of at least 1:2, meaning that the potential profit is at least twice the potential loss. This allows traders to have a higher probability of making profits over the long term, even if not all trades are successful.

The risk/reward ratio is just one aspect of a trader's risk management strategy, which also includes setting stop-loss and take-profit orders, managing position sizes, and considering market conditions and other factors. Traders should always consider their risk tolerance and financial goals when determining their risk/reward ratio and overall risk management strategy.

Position sizing and money management

Position sizing and money management are key elements of a successful forex trading strategy. Position sizing refers to determining the appropriate amount of currency to trade based on the size of the trading account, risk tolerance, and market conditions. Money management refers to the overall strategy for managing trading capital, including risk management, position sizing, and other considerations.

Position sizing involves calculating the appropriate trade size based on the trader's risk tolerance and the potential risk and reward of the trade. Traders should consider the size of their trading account, the potential profit and loss of the trade, and the risk/reward ratio when determining the appropriate trade size. It is generally recommended that traders limit their risk exposure to a certain percentage of their account balance, such as 1-2%.

Money management involves more than just position sizing and risk management. Traders should also consider diversifying their trading strategies and using different instruments and markets to reduce their risk exposure. Traders should also have a plan for withdrawing profits and managing losses over the long term.

One common money management technique is the use of a trading plan or strategy. A trading plan outlines the trader's goals, risk management strategy, and other considerations that may affect trading decisions. It also includes guidelines for position sizing, stop-loss and take-profit orders, and other aspects of trading.

Traders should also consider their emotional and psychological state when managing their trading capital. They should avoid trading on emotion or making impulsive decisions based on short-term market fluctuations. Instead, traders should focus on their long-term goals and use sound money management practices to help achieve those goals.

Overall, effective position sizing and money management are essential for long-term success in forex trading. Traders should develop a clear understanding of their risk tolerance and financial goals and use proven money management strategies to achieve those goals.

Trading psychology and emotional control

Trading psychology and emotional control are critical factors that can impact the success of a forex trader. Trading psychology refers to the mental and emotional aspects of trading, including the attitudes, beliefs, and behavior of the trader.

Emotions such as fear, greed, and anxiety can influence a trader's decision-making process and lead to impulsive and irrational trading decisions. To succeed in forex trading, traders must learn to control their emotions and make rational decisions based on a well-defined trading plan and strategy.

One of the most important aspects of trading psychology is having the right mindset. Traders should approach trading with a positive attitude and a willingness to learn and improve their skills. They should also have realistic expectations and understand that trading involves risks and losses, as well as profits.

Another important aspect of trading psychology is developing a trading plan and strategy that fits the trader's personality and risk tolerance. This includes setting clear goals, defining the risk/reward ratio, and using appropriate risk management techniques.

To control emotions while trading, traders can use various techniques, such as mindfulness and meditation, deep breathing exercises, and taking breaks to clear their minds. It is also important to avoid trading when feeling emotional or stressed and to stick to the trading plan and strategy.

Finally, traders should also learn from their mistakes and use them as opportunities to improve their skills and strategies. Keeping a trading journal can help traders analyze their trades, identify mistakes, and make adjustments to their trading plan.

In summary, trading psychology and emotional control are essential components of successful forex trading. By developing a positive mindset, using a well-defined trading plan and strategy, and learning to control their emotions, traders can increase their chances of success and achieve their long-term trading goals.

Chapter 6: Trading strategies

Trend-following strategies

Trend-following strategies are a popular approach to forex trading that aim to profit from trends in the currency markets. The basic idea behind a trend-following strategy is to identify the direction of the trend and trade in the same direction, with the goal of capturing as much of the trend as possible.

There are several indicators and tools that traders use to identify trends, including moving averages, trend lines, and price action patterns. The most common type of trend-following strategy is the moving average crossover strategy, which involves using two or more moving averages to identify the direction of the trend.

In a moving average crossover strategy, traders look for a crossover between a short-term moving average (such as a 20-day moving average) and a long-term moving average (such as a 50-day moving average). When the short-term moving average crosses above the long-term moving average, it is considered a buy signal, indicating that the trend is up. Conversely, when the short-term moving average crosses below the long-term moving average, it is considered a sell signal, indicating that the trend is down.

Another popular trend-following strategy is the use of trend lines. Trend lines are diagonal lines that connect two or more price points on a chart, and they can be used to identify the direction of the trend and potential support and resistance levels. When the price is above the trend line, it is considered an uptrend, and when it is below the trend line, it is considered a downtrend.

Price action patterns can also be used to identify trends and potential trade opportunities. Examples of price action patterns include higher highs and higher lows in an uptrend, and lower highs and lower lows in a downtrend.

One important consideration when using trend-following strategies is to be aware of potential false breakouts and reversals. Traders should always use appropriate risk management techniques, such as setting stop-loss orders and using appropriate position sizing and money management, to manage their risk and protect their trading capital.

In summary, trend-following strategies are a popular approach to forex trading that aim to profit from trends in the currency markets. By using indicators and tools to identify trends and potential trade opportunities, traders can increase their chances of success and achieve their long-term trading goals.

Range-trading strategies

Range-trading strategies are another approach to forex trading that involves trading within a range-bound market. Range-bound markets occur when the price of a currency pair moves within a certain price range, with support and resistance levels acting as boundaries for the price movement.

Range-trading strategies aim to identify these support and resistance levels and trade within the range. Traders will typically buy near the support level and sell near the resistance level, with the expectation that the price will continue to move within the range.

One common indicator used in range-trading strategies is the Relative Strength Index (RSI), which measures the strength of a currency pair's price action. Traders will look for oversold conditions near the support level and overbought conditions near the resistance level, and use the RSI to confirm these conditions.

Another approach to range-trading strategies is to use Bollinger Bands, which are bands plotted two standard deviations away from a simple moving average. The upper and lower bands act as potential resistance and support levels, and traders will look for price action near these levels to make trading decisions.

One important consideration when using range-trading strategies is to be aware of potential false breakouts and trends. Traders should always use appropriate risk management techniques, such as setting stop-loss orders and using appropriate position sizing and money management, to manage their risk and protect their trading capital.

In summary, range-trading strategies involve trading within a range-bound market by identifying support and resistance levels and buying near support and selling near resistance. By using indicators such as the RSI and Bollinger Bands to identify potential trade opportunities, traders can increase their chances of success and achieve their long-term trading goals.

Breakout strategies

Breakout strategies are a popular approach to forex trading that involve identifying and trading price breakouts above or below key levels of support or resistance. A price breakout occurs when the price of a currency pair breaks through a significant support or resistance level, indicating a potential change in trend.

Traders using breakout strategies will typically wait for the price to break through a key support or resistance level before entering a trade in the direction of the breakout. This strategy aims to capture large price movements that can occur after a breakout, potentially resulting in significant profits.

One common approach to breakout strategies is to use technical indicators such as moving averages or Bollinger Bands to identify potential breakout levels. Traders will look for price action that breaks through these levels and enter a trade in the direction of the breakout, with a stop-loss order placed below the breakout level to manage risk.

Another approach to breakout strategies is to use price action analysis to identify key support and resistance levels, and enter a trade when the price breaks through these levels. This approach may be more subjective, but can be effective for experienced traders who are able to identify key levels based on their understanding of market dynamics and price trends.

One important consideration when using breakout strategies is to be aware of false breakouts, where the price breaks through a key level but then quickly retraces back within the range. Traders should always use appropriate risk management techniques, such as setting stop-loss orders and using appropriate position sizing and money management, to manage their risk and protect their trading capital.

In summary, breakout strategies involve identifying and trading price breakouts above or below key levels of support or resistance. By using technical indicators or price action analysis to identify potential breakout levels, traders can increase their chances of success and achieve their long-term trading goals.

Swing trading strategies

Swing trading is a trading strategy that aims to capture medium-term price movements in the forex market, typically over a few days to a few weeks. This approach involves identifying and trading the swings or price movements that occur within a larger trend.

Swing traders will typically use a combination of technical analysis and fundamental analysis to identify potential trading opportunities. They may use technical indicators such as moving averages, trend lines, and chart patterns to identify trends and potential reversal points, as well as fundamental analysis to identify economic factors that may affect the market.

One common approach to swing trading is to identify key levels of support and resistance, and enter a trade when the price bounces off these levels. Traders will typically set a stop-loss order below the support level or above the resistance level, and aim to take profit at the next key level of support or resistance.

Another approach to swing trading is to use technical indicators to identify trend reversals. Traders may use indicators such as the Relative Strength Index (RSI) or the Moving Average Convergence Divergence (MACD) to identify potential reversal points, and enter a trade in the direction of the new trend.

Swing trading can be an effective strategy for traders who have a longer-term outlook and are willing to hold positions for several days or weeks. It can also be less stressful than day trading, as traders have more time to analyze the market and make trading decisions.

One important consideration when using swing trading strategies is to manage risk effectively. Traders should use appropriate position sizing, set stop-loss orders to limit losses, and aim for a favorable risk-reward ratio in each trade.

In summary, swing trading is a trading strategy that aims to capture medium-term price movements in the forex market. By using technical analysis and fundamental analysis to identify potential trading opportunities, and managing risk effectively, traders can increase their chances of success and achieve their long-term trading goals.

Chapter 7: Developing a Trading plan

Setting trading goals

Setting trading goals is an important part of developing a successful trading strategy. A trading goal is a specific, measurable objective that a trader sets for themselves in order to achieve success in the markets. Without clear goals, traders may find it difficult to stay motivated and may be more likely to make impulsive or emotional trading decisions.

The first step in setting trading goals is to define what success means to you. This could involve setting a specific profit target, achieving a certain level of consistency in your trading, or simply learning to trade with discipline and patience.

Once you have defined your overall trading goal, you can then break it down into smaller, more specific objectives. For example, you may set a goal to achieve a certain level of profitability each month, or to increase your win rate by a certain percentage.

It is also important to set goals that are realistic and achievable. Traders who set unrealistic goals may become discouraged when they are unable to achieve them, and may be more likely to take on excessive risk or make impulsive trading decisions.

In addition to setting goals, it is important to develop a trading plan that outlines the specific steps you will take to achieve your objectives. This may involve identifying specific trading strategies that you will use, setting risk management guidelines, and developing a daily routine that will help you stay focused and disciplined.

Finally, it is important to regularly review your trading goals and adjust them as necessary. As you gain experience and become more familiar with the markets, you may find that your goals and objectives change. By regularly reviewing and adjusting your goals, you can ensure that you stay motivated and continue to make progress towards achieving long-term success in your trading.

Defining a trading strategy

Defining a trading strategy is essential for achieving success in the markets. A trading strategy is a set of rules and guidelines that a trader follows in order to make informed trading decisions. A well-defined trading strategy can help traders to minimize risk, maximize profits, and achieve their trading goals.

The first step in defining a trading strategy is to determine your trading style. This could be day trading, swing trading, or position trading, among others. Your trading style will dictate the types of trades you make, as well as the time frame in which you hold positions.

Once you have determined your trading style, you can then begin to develop a set of rules for entering and exiting trades. This may involve identifying key technical indicators or chart patterns that signal a potential trade opportunity, as well as setting specific price levels for entering and exiting positions.

In addition to entry and exit rules, a trading strategy should also include guidelines for managing risk. This may involve setting stop-loss orders to limit potential losses, or using position sizing and money management techniques to ensure that you are not risking more than you can afford to lose.

Another important aspect of a trading strategy is to have a plan for dealing with unexpected market events or changes in market conditions. This could involve setting rules for adjusting your trading plan based on new information or market developments, or simply being prepared to adapt to changing market conditions as needed.

Finally, it is important to regularly review and refine your trading strategy based on your experiences in the markets. By continually assessing your trading performance and making adjustments to your strategy as necessary, you can increase your chances of long-term success in the markets.

Backtesting and forward testing

Backtesting and forward testing are essential components of developing and refining a trading strategy.

Backtesting involves using historical market data to test a trading strategy's performance. Traders can use software programs or manually analyze the data to determine how the strategy would have performed under different market conditions. By analyzing the historical performance of a trading strategy, traders can identify potential weaknesses or strengths and make adjustments accordingly.

Forward testing, on the other hand, involves using a trading strategy in real-time market conditions to see how it performs. This involves placing actual trades based on the strategy and tracking the results. Forward testing can provide valuable insights into how the strategy performs under current market conditions and can help traders to refine their strategy further.

When backtesting a trading strategy, it is important to use a large and diverse dataset to ensure that the results are statistically significant. The dataset should also include a range of market conditions, such as bullish, bearish, and volatile markets.

Forward testing is typically done with a smaller set of trades than backtesting, as it involves placing actual trades in the live market. Traders can use a demo account to test the strategy without risking real money, or they can use a small amount of capital to test the strategy in a live trading account.

It is important to note that while backtesting and forward testing can provide valuable insights into a trading strategy's performance, they cannot guarantee future success. Market conditions are always changing, and a trading strategy that performs well in backtesting or forward testing may not necessarily perform well in the future. As such, it is important to regularly review and refine your trading strategy based on current market conditions and your own experiences in the markets.

Keeping a trading journal

Keeping a trading journal is an essential part of becoming a successful trader. It is a record of your trading activities and can provide valuable insights into your performance and help you improve your trading skills.

A trading journal should include the following information:

Date and time of the trade
Type of trade (buy or sell)
Trading instrument (currency pair, stock, etc.)
Entry price and exit price
Stop-loss and take-profit levels
Position size
Reason for entering the trade
Market conditions and any news or events that may have influenced the trade
Outcome of the trade (profit or loss)
Lessons learned from the trade
By recording this information for each trade, you can identify patterns in your trading behavior, track your progress over time, and make adjustments to your trading strategy based on your performance.

In addition to the information listed above, you may also want to include notes on your emotions during the trade.

This can help you identify any emotional biases that may be affecting your decision-making process and allow you to develop strategies for managing your emotions while trading.

Reviewing your trading journal regularly can help you identify areas where you need to improve and track your progress over time. It can also help you avoid making the same mistakes repeatedly and make adjustments to your trading strategy based on your experiences in the market.

In conclusion, keeping a trading journal is an essential tool for traders looking to improve their skills and become more successful in the markets. By recording your trading activities and reviewing them regularly, you can gain valuable insights into your performance and make adjustments to your strategy accordingly.

Chapter 8: Choosing a Broker and Trading platform

Key considerations for choosing a forex broker

Choosing the right forex broker is crucial for any trader, as it can impact your trading experience and ultimately affect your bottom line. Here are some key considerations to keep in mind when selecting a forex broker:

Regulation: One of the most important factors to consider when choosing a forex broker is their regulatory status. Look for brokers that are regulated by reputable organizations such as the Financial Conduct Authority (FCA) in the UK, the National Futures Association (NFA) in the US, or the Australian Securities and Investments Commission (ASIC).

Trading platform: The trading platform provided by the broker is another important consideration. Look for a platform that is user-friendly, stable, and offers a range of tools and features to help you analyze the markets and make informed trading decisions.

Customer service: Make sure the broker offers good customer service and support, including responsive customer support and a range of contact options such as phone, email, and live chat.

Trading costs: Trading costs can have a significant impact on your profitability, so it's important to choose a broker that offers competitive spreads and low commission fees.

Deposits and withdrawals: Look for a broker that offers a range of payment options and fast and secure deposits and withdrawals.

Educational resources: The best forex brokers offer a range of educational resources such as webinars, tutorials, and trading guides to help you improve your trading skills and knowledge.

Reputation: Finally, make sure you choose a broker with a good reputation in the industry. Look for brokers with positive reviews from other traders and a track record of reliability and trustworthiness.

By considering these key factors when selecting a forex broker, you can help ensure that you choose a broker that meets your needs and provides a positive trading experience.

Demo trading and live trading accounts

Demo trading accounts and live trading accounts are two different types of accounts that forex brokers offer to their clients.

A demo account is a simulated trading environment that allows traders to practice trading without risking any real money. These accounts are usually free and come with virtual funds that can be used to simulate trading conditions in the live markets. Demo accounts are an excellent way for beginners to learn how to trade and for experienced traders to test new strategies without risking real money.

On the other hand, a live trading account is a real trading account that is used to trade with real money. To open a live account, traders must deposit real money into their account, which they can then use to trade in the live markets. Live accounts offer traders the opportunity to make real profits, but also come with the risk of real losses.

There are several key differences between demo trading and live trading accounts. Firstly, trading conditions on a demo account may not accurately reflect the real trading conditions that you will experience on a live account. For example, spreads, slippage, and execution times may differ between the two account types.

Another difference between demo and live trading accounts is the psychological impact of trading with real money. Trading with real money can cause emotions such as fear, greed, and excitement to come into play, which can affect your decision-making and trading performance. In contrast, demo trading allows traders to practice without the emotional pressure that comes with trading real money.

Overall, demo trading and live trading accounts serve different purposes. Demo accounts are great for learning and testing strategies, while live accounts are for trading with real money and making profits. Traders should use both types of accounts to get the most out of their trading experience.

Popular trading platforms and tools

There are many different trading platforms and tools available for forex traders. Here are some of the most popular ones:

MetaTrader 4 (MT4) and MetaTrader 5 (MT5): These are two of the most widely used trading platforms in the forex market. They offer a range of features, including advanced charting tools, customizable indicators, and the ability to automate trading strategies.

cTrader: This is a popular trading platform that offers advanced charting tools and a range of order types, including limit orders and stop orders.

TradingView: This is a popular charting platform that offers real-time data and advanced charting tools. It also offers a social community where traders can share ideas and collaborate with each other.

Forex Factory: This is a website that offers a range of tools and resources for forex traders, including a calendar of economic events, trading forums, and market analysis.

Economic calendars: These are tools that provide information on upcoming economic events that could affect the forex market, such as interest rate decisions and employment reports.

Trading robots: These are automated trading systems that use algorithms to enter and exit trades. They can be programmed to follow specific trading strategies and can help traders save time and reduce emotional decision-making.

Trading signals: These are alerts that provide traders with information on potential trading opportunities. They can be generated by human analysts or by automated trading systems.

Overall, the choice of trading platform and tools will depend on your individual trading style and needs. It's important to research and test different options to find the ones that work best for you.

Chapter 9: Conclusion

Review of key concepts and strategies

In this book on forex trading for beginners, we covered a range of key concepts and strategies that are important to understand when trading in the forex market. Here is a review of the main topics we covered:

What is forex trading: We started by defining what forex trading is and how it works. We explained that it involves buying and selling currency pairs and that the aim is to profit from changes in exchange rates.

Advantages and risks of forex trading: We discussed the advantages of forex trading, such as its liquidity and the ability to trade 24 hours a day, as well as the risks, such as market volatility and leverage.

History of forex trading: We explored the history of forex trading, from its origins in the gold standard to the modern forex market.

Currency pairs and exchange rates: We explained how currency pairs are quoted and how exchange rates are determined.

Pips and pipettes: We discussed the concept of pips and pipettes and how they are used to measure price movements in the forex market.

Lot sizes and leverage: We explored the concept of lot sizes and leverage and how they can be used to control the size of trades.

Margin and margin calls: We explained the concept of margin and how it is used to trade with leverage. We also discussed the risks of margin trading and how margin calls work.

Economic indicators and news releases: We explored how economic indicators and news releases can impact currency markets and how traders can use this information to make trading decisions.

Technical analysis: We discussed the use of technical analysis in forex trading, including candlestick charts, trend lines, support and resistance levels, and common technical indicators.

Trading strategies: We explored different trading strategies, including trend-following strategies, range-trading strategies, breakout strategies, and swing trading strategies.

Trading psychology and emotional control: We emphasized the importance of maintaining emotional control when trading and discussed techniques for managing emotions and setting trading goals.

Choosing a forex broker: We discussed key considerations when choosing a forex broker, including regulatory oversight, trading platforms, and customer support.

Demo trading and live trading accounts: We explored the benefits of demo trading and how it can be used to practice trading strategies without risking real money. We also discussed the differences between demo and live trading accounts.

Popular trading platforms and tools: We discussed some of the most popular trading platforms and tools used by forex traders, including MetaTrader 4 and 5, cTrader, TradingView, economic calendars, trading robots, and trading signals.

Overall, this book aimed to provide beginners with a comprehensive introduction to forex trading, covering both key concepts and practical strategies. By understanding these concepts and strategies, readers should be better equipped to start trading in the forex market with confidence.

Next steps for beginner traders

Congratulations! You have now learned about the fundamentals of forex trading, including its advantages and risks, currency pairs and exchange rates, lot sizes and leverage, technical indicators, trading psychology, and trading strategies.

As a beginner trader, your next steps should include practicing your skills and developing your trading plan. Here are some recommended next steps:

Open a demo trading account: Most reputable forex brokers offer free demo accounts that allow you to practice trading with virtual funds. This is a great way to get a feel for the markets and test out different trading strategies without risking real money.

Develop your trading plan: Based on the strategies and concepts you have learned, develop a detailed trading plan that outlines your goals, risk management strategies, and entry and exit criteria.

Backtest your trading plan: Use historical data to test your trading plan and see how it would have performed in the past. This can help you identify any weaknesses in your plan and make adjustments before trading with real money.

Start trading with a small amount of money: Once you have tested your trading plan and feel comfortable, start trading with a small amount of money. This will allow you to gain real-world trading experience while minimizing your risk.

Continuously monitor and evaluate your performance: Keep a trading journal to track your trades and evaluate your performance over time. Use this information to make adjustments to your trading plan as needed.

Remember, forex trading is a journey that requires continuous learning and adaptation. Stay committed to your goals and continue to educate yourself about the markets, and you can become a successful forex trader. Good luck!

Additional resources for learning and improvement

There are many resources available for beginner forex traders who want to continue learning and improving their skills. Here are some additional resources to consider:

Online courses: Many online courses are available that cover the fundamentals of forex trading and advanced trading strategies. These courses may include video lectures, quizzes, and interactive exercises.

Trading forums: Joining online trading forums can be a great way to connect with other traders, ask questions, and learn from their experiences.

Books: There are many books available on forex trading that cover a range of topics from the basics to advanced strategies. Some popular titles include "Currency Trading for Dummies" by Kathleen Brooks and Brian Dolan, "Technical Analysis of the Financial Markets" by John J. Murphy, and "Trading in the Zone" by Mark Douglas.

Webinars: Many brokers and trading experts offer free webinars that cover various topics related to forex trading. These can be a great way to learn from experts and ask questions in real-time.

Trading simulators: Some trading platforms offer trading simulators that allow you to practice trading with virtual funds in real-time market conditions.

News and analysis: Staying up-to-date on economic news and analysis can help you make informed trading decisions. Consider subscribing to financial news websites, following market analysts on social media, and regularly reading financial publications.

Remember, the key to success in forex trading is continuous learning and improvement. Make use of the resources available to you, stay disciplined, and continuously evaluate and refine your trading plan.